LYNNE COLEMAN is an author and bro⟶
fashion. For over a decad⟶
as Burberry, Chanel, Céli⟶
Luxury is listened to in 40
across the textiles sector ir
oldest artisan tartan mill, I

This is Lynne's fourth book

Front cover illustration of Grace Kelly wearing Pringle of Scotland

By the same author:

A Girl's Guide to Vintage, Luath Press, 2010
Cashmere: A Guide to Scottish Luxury, Luath Press, 2017
The Fashion Annual, Luath Press, 2018

How Scotland Dressed The World

LYNNE COLEMAN

Luath Press Limited

EDINBURGH

www.luath.co.uk

First published 2021

ISBN: 978-1-910022-87-0

The author's right to be identified as author of this book
under the Copyright, Designs and Patents Act 1988 has been asserted.

The paper used in this book is recyclable. It is made
from low chlorine pulps produced in a low energy,
low emission manner from renewable forests.

Printed and bound by
iPrint Global Ltd., Ely

Typeset in 11 point FreightTextPro by
Eilidh MacLennan

Dedicated to Jamie, Gabriel, Rafe and Ruben

CONTENTS

This is my
love letter to
a nation that
gives us the
blueprint for
international
style.

INTRODUCTION

For over a decade, I've worked with brands such as Burberry and Mulberry. I've had my breath taken away sitting cheek by jowl at Chanel's Métiers d'Art show and I've pulled my pick of the high street on a weekly basis for the fashion pages of the *Edinburgh Evening News* and *Scotland on Sunday*, all the while penning a monthly style column for *Town & Country*.

This was all done in tandem with working across the textiles sector here in Scotland, as Brand Guardian of our oldest artisan tartan mill – DC Dalgliesh – and amassing the largest personal library of tartan on the planet, with swatches sourced from all the weaving mills in my homeland. So, as you can see, my research credentials are pretty rock solid.

Between publications, runways and a plethora of press dinners in every fashion capital, one thing became abundantly clear: Scotland's impact on style around the world is so huge that I began seeing a pattern in trends that would lead me straight back to our bonnie, bonnie banks.

From the rebellion of 1745 – when the Jacobites flooded battlefields – to the dismantling of the movement a year later that resulted in our national dress being banned, to its regal reinstating by George IV 200 years ago, this book marks the bicentenary of a movement that solidified Scotland's style credentials.

Our fabric is the storyteller of fashion, the yarn-spinner of clothing. It tells you a tale as soon as you lay eyes on it. We go to war in the stuff and marry in it – how wonderful to wander around in this walking contradiction of a cloth.

These fibres are soaked in gasoline levels of storytelling, so flammable it has ignited the hearts and imaginations of the masses around the world. The beauty of it all is that you don't have to be Scottish to aspire to its aesthetic.

From punk to preppy, romance to royalty, gothic to grunge, these were trends that I continually saw getting regurgitated on runways and shop floors alike. And it was here that I began seeing the pattern leading back to Scotland every season.

Don't just take my word for it, come and see how Scotland has remained part of the zeitgeist by diving into the pages of *How Scotland Dressed the World*. Find out how that chic Parisian vibe starts off at the tweed mills of the Scottish Borders. How that impeccable

Italian aesthetic is set off with Scottish cashmere. And how America has harnessed preppy dressing through weaving at our tartan mills. I even throw in a few Scottish phrases for your reading pleasure, because there is nothing more delicious than the Scots language, especially when it's about dressing. This is my love letter to a nation that gives us the blueprint for international style.

SCOTLAND I SALUTE YOU

Lynne Coleman

GALLUS

Pronunciation / Ga-lass

ADJECTIVE

Scottish

1. *bold*

2. *cheeky*

3. *flashy*

WORD ORIGIN
comes from the word gallows used as an adjective,
meaning 'fit for the gallows'

Gallus is an informal term used to describe an act of boldness or daring eg. 'He was being a wee bit gallus with Mrs McDonald, luckily for him she likes a laugh!'

You are implying that someone is doing something cheeky when deploying this word.

In contemporary terms, it can also refer to someone who does something in a stylish or flawless way. Quite a turnaround for an adjective that would nowadays sooner see you wearing a killer fit than a noose.

Isolated Heroes is in my opinion, hands down the most gallus label in Scotland. Sam McEwan started Isolated Heroes a decade ago and she's been serving us luxury faux furs and sassy sequins ever since.

Her incredible team have grown to become one of the most visually striking contemporary brands in the country dressing celebrities such as Miley Cyrus, Paloma Faith, Pixie Lott, Kate Nash and Molly King, and a number of high profile influencers including Tess Holliday, Danielle Vanier, Sophie Hannah Richardson and the Confetti Crowd. However, it's her everyday customers that really bring the gallus!

Where did you get that outfit? It's pure gallus!

ROMANCE

NOUN

1. *a sense of excitement and mystery that comes with being in love.*

2. *a sense or feeling of mystery, excitement, and difference from normal life.*

'Above, there is a bright star near the last of the pink-edged seed moon. And there she is, lying on the lavender where the housemaids spread the laundry.'
from *The Fair Botanist* by Sara Sheridan

Scotland's strong hold over romance can clearly be seen with *Outlander*. What's more romantic than castles, kilts and luscious rolling scenery?

At the turn of the new decade, visitors were up by 200 per cent at Doune Castle, near Stirling. Researchers at Glasgow Caledonian University studied the Outlander effect on 25 of the show's locations across Scotland and saw a 45 per cent rise in visitors to the sites over four years, which they say is 'well in excess' of increases experienced at other Scottish attractions. And what of the legions of fans who can't get here? Well, they settle in to watching the show wrapped in wool blankets and cashmere socks, with a whisky cocktail in hand. When a new season streams, we see a surge in sales across America and Europe for such items. It's not lost on me that the spike coincides with the buzz of a new season streaming online.

In particular, I want to tell tartan's story in a way we haven't heard before. We all know of its ability to connect people by name. But much like the warp and weft of the fabric's weave and plethora of parallel lines, it also retains the ability to tell stories.

Most recently, it has become the focus of one of my biggest labours of love – my tartan archive.

Gathering the archive has taken me to tartan mills round the country: from Harris to Elgin, Bute to

Selkirk and Langholm to Glasgow, before finally taking up residency on our bookshelves.

After I had amassed a Ben Nevis-sized amount of fabric, the fear of losing everything to moths got real. I sourced vintage 1950s glass display cabinets, encasing the colossal collection for its own safety.

As I put away endless swatches, kilt-ends, remnants, scarves and stoles, it dawned on me that I'd accumulated the largest personal tartan library on the planet – around 10,000 pieces.

The reason for casting my net so wide was simple: I wanted to source fabric from all over Scotland to create mini collections illustrating how tartan has infiltrated trends and created zeitgeists – how it has the ability to act as an adopted symbol for so many recognisable movements throughout history.

From punk to preppy, royalty to romance, gothic to grunge and spanning conservatism to rebellion, Scottish textiles have managed to wrap themselves around individual bodies, homes, brands, corporations, sporting institutions and even armies over the years, while still retaining an edgy aloofness.

This idea led me down a rabbit hole of research, uncovering themes I'd not heard in more than a decade of working in this domain. My current

favourite description of tartan is as 'the floral garden', a turn of phrase about my national dress that struck me as perfectly apt.

In 1723, the author of *A Journey Through Scotland*, John Macky, described women wearing tartan in church as a *'parterre de fleurs'*, a little gem I discovered inside Ian Brown's tome From *Tartan to Tartantry*.

Brown draws on this thread to move into a discussion of wedding attire, of morning dress versus the kilt. In conversation with an academic friend whose daughter is about to walk down the aisle, he learns that the bride has persuaded her father out of the former and into the latter – a style swap he is thankful for, lest he end up looking like 'a penguin in a flower garden'.

It felt fitting to be surrounded by such fragrant language as I read and archived. The blooms from my own floral garden, tangled up in the place where I house my plaid, now seem like the perfect jumping-off point for my text and textile journey.

However, it's the link between the New Romantics of the late 1970s and early 1980s and the Romanticism movement between 1800 and 1850 that tickles me most. While Sir Walter Scott was aggressively wooing royalty (more on that in the regal section) and the Enlightenment swept the globe, parallels between people wanting intellectual escapism rapidly spilled into the physical. With a wave of new art, music, inventions and literature came the want to own a slice of it, as a reaction to the harshness of the Industrial Revolution, much like the New Romantic movement was born in the UK out of the decline in industry and unrest caused by strikes bringing the country to a standstill.

The need for escapism exploded. Clothing and make-up became theatrical and bold; decadence and excess in both eras. Tartan was back with a bang after being made illegal during the 1745 rebellion, with people wanting to weave difficult colourways to flaunt their wealth. Red was the shade *du jour* as it was the hardest colour to create and the most expensive because they needed lots of different components to create the colour.

As I conjure thoughts of gigantic, ostentatious portraits of 200-year-old figures, my mind whips to a visual of David Bowie clad in tartan,

suited with freshly dyed ginger hair that looks like it's fizzing. Images of him then are like a mash-up of iconic Scottish women: Mary, Queen of Scots, with a slice of Tilda Swinton and a serving of Annie Lennox sporting a citric acid pixie cut. Perfection!

But just like a wave, the movement that started out with pure romantic intentions came crashing down. The Victorians swept away the vulgar excesses of the generation before them, adopting a more prudent way of life. Similarly, The Smiths and Nirvana took a sledgehammer to the excesses of Boy George and Duran Duran, in their peacocking silk plaids. And although the movement was set adrift, tartan still wound up on the backs of Kurt Cobain and Morrissey, ushering in the era of grunge and the joy of an oversized checked shirt, much like Queen Victoria claiming tartan as her own to create the Balmoral effect.

Back to the romance. In my opinion, the biggest impact Scotland has had on romance as a trend sits inside the bridal market. Formal Highland wear has been used in wedding ceremonies for centuries.

Often, people come to me asking which tartan their surname belongs to. The answer is never simple since there are many tartan variations under any given name. Even more beautiful, there's a tradition of creating brand new tartans when two families come together. That's one of the reasons you find so many differing patterns sharing the same surname. I may be showing my soppy side here, but I think that's ludicrously romantic. Through working with DC Dalgliesh, I have seen first-hand the enormous presence Scotland has on the global wedding market. We have shipped wedding kilts to over 120 countries around the globe and we are just one of several Scottish tartan mills, which blows my mind.

My final thought falls on the romantic trend which stole my heart, dubbed 'the cashmere wedding'. Think rustic outdoor settings and blankets over chairs to keep guests warm. Butter-soft cashmere stoles over silky bridesmaid dresses. Flowers sprayed everywhere, colours popping with tartan. Special weave cashmere kilts teamed with chunky cable knits. It looks authentically homemade but oozes luxury with every tactile touch. What's not to love?

PEELY-WALLY

ADJECTIVE

Scottish

1. *Pale and off-colour*

2. *Looking unwell and tired*

'wally' pronounced rally, not holly.

*'Think you might need some Fake Bake hen,
you're looking awfy peely-wally.'*

Danish photographer Eva Rødbro and Swedish artist Charlott Markus created Tableau Noir, building an abstract room and covering everything in herringbone Harris Tweed. I had the pleasure of creating a pictorial using the room as a backdrop a few years ago. The artists had been inspired by the darkness of Scottish literature, so it was easy to push this concept further by injecting an *Alice in Wonderland* narrative around the work. I wanted hair and make-up to conjure the Queen of Hearts, while our model played Alice after consuming the 'drink me' potion, a nod to *Jekyll and Hyde* references made by the duo. But it also allowed me some tongue-in-cheek fun, with the phrase 'peely-wally' played out in pictures.

I opted to style everything in monochrome textured fabric to mirror the room.

The Max Mara cashmere coat was such a dreamy combination. I also adored the giant font shift dress by Moschino. Marrying Italian fashion with this was the cherry on top of this artistic sundae. Nuala Swan captured the images on film, adding another atmospheric layer to everything.

The fabric was donated by the Harris Tweed Authority and formed part of the programme for 2014's *Edinburgh International Fashion Festival*.

An admiration for Scots author James Hogg's seminal work *The Private Memoirs and Confessions of a Justified Sinner* and Robert Louis Stevenson's *The Strange Case of Dr Jekyll and Mr Hyde* were successfully fused into classic film noir. This editorial is a celebration of that.

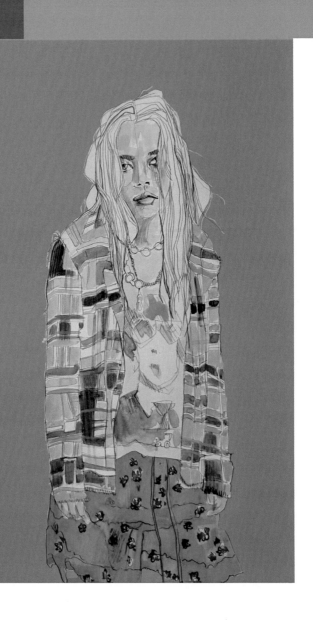

GRUNGE

NOUN

grunge rock; plural noun: grunge rocks

1. *grime, dirt*

2. *a type of rock music exemplified by a harsh, loud guitar sound and lazy vocals.*

3. *the fashion style that goes with the grunge genre. typically shown through loose layers and ripped jeans.*

Now, the story I'm about to share links Kurt Cobain with Dennis the Menace and got Marc Jacobs fired.

Standing in a striped jumper, Kurt Cobain became the poster child of grunge with his unwashed hair, stretched check shirts, misshapen knits, battered jeans and worn-out trainers forming the blueprint uniform of a generation.

This was a natural evolution from punk, the ultimate 'I couldn't give a f**k what I'm wearing' attitude that halved the time it took to get ready. Punks typically styled their hair, wore lots of accessories and added make-up for a more theatrical approach. Grunge was the antithesis of this. It flipped the bird to the trend that famously stuck two fingers up to the establishment.

The irony in the movement always tickles me. After all, it still uses clothing as a tool to express a feeling, providing a mirror to society about what is happening culturally and economically, carried on the back of the wearer.

There was extreme fatigue coming off the back of 1980s excess. Big hair and shoulder pads gave way to slick locks and shift dresses. Grunge showed us this on the fashion frontlines.

Now our link back to Scotland via Seattle doesn't come from Cobain being born in Aberdeen, or even attending Aberdeen High School. That's Aberdeen, Washington, and not the oil rich shores of the 'shire. But you get my tenuous drift.

This story is grungier than that.

In the summer of 1992, Nirvana played at the King's Hall in Belfast. That night, a local lad called Chris Black from Whitehead went to the gig wearing a black and red Dennis the Menace jumper. Courtney Love clocked it and began bartering to buy it. She loved it and wanted to gift it to Kurt (let's be honest, she has the best taste in the world). Reluctantly, Chris parted with the sweater for £35, selling it to a jubilant Love. The tale has been retold in newspapers and on radio programmes ever since.

From there, the musician was pictured in Dennis the

Menace's pullover a plethora of times.

The symbolism of Cobain cocooned inside Dennis's attire is not lost on me. What that character represents – a lost little boy adored by the world but who impacts his loved ones on a daily basis with naughty self-indulgent behaviour – is a poetic microcosm. I have no idea if Love knew the Dennis the Menace backstory when she bought it, but this piece of parabolic paraphernalia certainly has more weight added to it knowing that she chose it.

By the time winter rolled round that year, a young Marc Jacobs sent a collection down the runway that critics scoffed at. Why? you may ask. Well, he'd been brought into Perry Ellis fresh out of Parsons to inject some youthful ideas into their stuttering sportswear line. Things weren't really running to plan. The final nail in his coffin

came when he sent Christy Turlington, Kate Moss and Kristen McMenamy, along with the rest of the Supers, strutting down the catwalk in Cobain-inspired clobber. Looking at it today, the collection was utter genius. But, it was far too cool for the stuffy old farts that he was presenting to that day. Bias-cut tartan skirts teamed with cute cartoon t-shirts and finished with loose shirts and knitted beanies; it looked like Scotland-the-chic, but fashion writers condemned it. They stated that he'd raided Seattle's thrift stores and hardcore grunge lovers hurtled hatred at him, accusing him of selling out their beloved movement.

I say, utter bollocks to that. Jacobs had his finger on the pulse of a movement, an ability that would allow him to rise from the ashes like a fashion phoenix after he was fired from his post. With a few knit beanies and silk negligees, Jacobs had tapped into the zeitgeist of Kurt Cobain and Courtney Love, thus catapulting the subculture to the forefront of style. Ultimately, the grunge show would mark a turning point in fashion: the definitive transition from couture houses to street style happen right there on Marc Jacob's watch.

And in case you are unaware of the origins of Dennis the Menace, he is one of the most famous characters to come out of DC Thomson – the publishing powerhouse that hails from Dundee. But back to Jacobs...

Fast forward to the present day and there isn't a fashionista worth her salt who doesn't know Marc's name. His impact on popular culture has been firmly felt for three decades. And what of that infamous wee jumper? Well, Jacobs has brought out different variations of The Grunge Sweater by Marc Jacobs over the years. In 2018, he marked the 25th anniversary of the dreaded Perry Ellis collection by recapturing the vibe. It would prove another controversial move, with the surviving members of Nirvana suing Jacobs for a reimagined version of their smiley face Nevermind logo, resulting in a countersuit from Team Jacobs. Someone should remind them if anyone should be hacked-off for style stealing its poor wee Dennis.

But back to Chris Black and the jumper. He has said in the press he'd love the opportunity to buy the piece and have it returned to him. I have no idea if that has ever manifested. If not, I think Marc Jacobs should send Chris one of his as a gift. After all, without Chris, Cobain and Dennis the Menace, his career could have turned out very differently.

TREWS

NOUN
plural noun: trews

Scottish

1. *trousers.*

2. *close–fitting tartan trousers,*
known to be worn by certain Scottish regiments.

WORD ORIGIN

thought to originate from the mid 16th century from
Irish triús, Scottish Gaelic triubhas.

A flash of red bundled inside a bargain bucket shot out like a beacon of light beneath a sea of beige fabric.

It had the same effect a flame has on a moth. Excitedly I fluttered over, bumping into the iron basket en route. It was 2008, I had just been made redundant and was self-soothing in the charity shops of Edinburgh's Gorgie Road. With silver shrapnel burning a hole in my pocket, the bargain bin felt like the best place to part with the last of my dosh. As I pulled the pair of trousers out, the Pringle of Scotland Faldo label flashed at me. I was giddy with excitement. The prospect of bagging Pringle for a pound was palpable! The fact they were 1980s synthetic golf trousers simply didn't matter. The close tartan set in red and navy was so chic I knew the trews-like nature of their voluminous material would look bloody brilliant styled out. So, I parted with a pound and took them home.

Seven years later, Pringle of Scotland turned 200. I was friends with one of the senior consultants who had cast another one of our friends in the campaign to celebrate the bicentenary. There was a full summer of festivities being held between Edinburgh, London and Milan. I had never told either of them the story of the trews until walking around the exhibition, one frosty evening on press preview night at London Fashion Week. As we walked and talked I shared the tale of the Faldo trews. Instantly, Benoit turned around to me and asked if they could buy back the trousers for their own archive as the business had never really catalogued old collections or memorabilia. The trousers appeared in my first book and had seen me through many a fashion evening with the brand, and had made TV appearances and been chatted about in several columns of mine, so I couldn't let them go. In his fabulous French accent, while handing over another glass of champagne, he playfully told me that he hated me but utterly understood. It was one of those perfect fashion night outs.

PREPPY

NOUN

1. *someone who goes to or has graduated from an expensive prep school, or a person who looks like a pupil of one in clothing or appearance.*

ADJECTIVE

1. *someone who behaves like a pupil or graduate of an expensive prep school, usually shown through their neat style of clothing.*

'The Preppy Look'

DEPENDING ON WHICH SIDE OF THE ATLANTIC YOU RESIDE WILL DETERMINE HOW YOU WEAR PREPPY.

I say this with a caveat: you can physically be anywhere on the planet but mentally you will resonate with one aesthetic over the other.

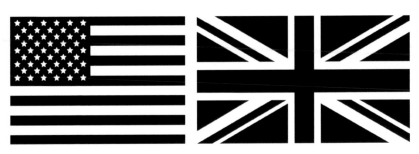

Molly Goddard AW21

This trend is two sides of the same style coin. However, Americans and Europeans like to express their differences with a few style tweaks that automatically show you who's a Sloane Ranger or an Ivy Leaguer. In my humble opinion, no one does preppy better than a Parisian. This Scot is a sucker for Chanel. Our Auld Alliance was built on many a burning issue, ranging from political to economic, but the trade between our creative industries is an unbreakable bond still going strong today. There isn't a couturier in Paris who doesn't have a Scottish mill on speed dial – but more on that later.

THE IVY LEAGUER

Think Ralph Lauren, OutKast and Pharrel Williams at the turn of the 21st century, or Diane Keaton at any decade and queens Dionne and Cher in *Clueless*. It's old Hollywood glamour, like Grace Kelly in *High Society* or Betty Draper in *Mad Men*.

THE SLOANE RANGER

Think Princess Diana in her 1980s heyday to Alexa Chung now. It's about pussy bows, pearls and Barbour jackets. Quintessentially British, with all that quilted quirk.

THE PARISIAN

Alaïa, Balmain, Celine, Chanel, Dior, Gaultier, Givenchy, Lanvin – the list goes on. What these couturiers do with tweed, tartan and knitwear, season after season, blows my mind. Their dedication to preppy persuasions is simply perfection. They are the keepers of the twinset.

Much has been written about Gabrielle Chanel's love affair with Scotland and our fabrics. In the Highlands, her hideaway home Rosehall Estate is now unlovingly crumbling, which I think is a national disgrace – she personally hand painted the wallpaper, for Christ's sake. It makes me want to weep! However, I'm not so much of a numpty to not understand the difficulties of the estate or what an endeavour it would be to take on. It's more than 500 acres of land. The house is humungous and needs its asking price, at least, spent on it again to make it habitable once more.

It's also an hour north of Inverness, which is not easy terrain to navigate. And with the average house price of neighbouring properties around £200,000, it makes the eye-watering price tag of £3 million seem a little hard to reach. The estate has been on and off the market for around a decade, with various parties showing interest then pulling out.

Despite difficulties during its heyday, Rosehall was loved. It provided the perfect amount of remoteness for Gabrielle to play out her romance with the Duke of Westminster, who resided there with her during their affair in the 1920s. Winston Churchill, a close friend of the Duke, recuperated on the estate around 1928 and letters about his stay have since been published.

According to the National Records of Scotland, Churchill remarked to his wife in one letter: 'She fishes from morning 'til night, and in two months has killed 50 salmon.'

The importance of this estate on Coco's inspiration and subsequent brand-building is not to be overlooked. This home formed the backbone of the woman she wanted to evolve into. The lady of the manor is quintessential Chanel. Tweeds and cashmeres fit to entertain in, (but still have an air of ease about them should you wish to fish) are really just polished ensembles of hunting gear around here. This is how Parisian Preppy was born.

It's a relationship that still thrives today, with Chanel owning Barrie Knitwear in the Scottish Borders.

From Paris to Hollywood…

Sailing on *True Love*, Grace Kelly and Bing Crosby serenade one another. It's a scene mid-movie from *High Society* that I never tire of watching. Kelly is wearing a powder pink cashmere twinset, beautifully belted in the middle and worn with a full skirt in a similar shade. Behind Bing sits a tartan blanket waiting patiently to be used whenever the moment should arise. But it never does. Obviously, the cashmere twinset was at the peak of its popularity in the 1950s, so you might want to argue that it would have been an obvious choice to have it involved in her costume design for this role.

That being said, there is a strong relationship at play here between our leading lady and one of Scotland's biggest textile giants. Kelly was a colossal cashmere fan. More than that, she was a loyal Pringle of Scotland customer too. It is said that she would celebrate momentous moments in her life by buying a twinset from the brand whenever she wanted to commemorate something. Usually, flying into their flagship store in New York to do so.

Several years ago, Central Saint Martins and Pringle of Scotland collaborated on a beautiful project celebrating their muse. Students from the school were allowed access to the princess's personal cashmere archive and designed a capsule that would eventually go on sale. The jumpers were incredible. My personal favourites had her name in intarsia on cobalt blue and grey cashmere sweaters.

This American mid-century prep-fest is the modern-day snapshot to how our Atlantic cousins consume their preppy. It's certainly the cornerstone of Ralph Lauren, and to me, the essence of their vibe. From Liv Tyler and Renée Zellweger in their tiny tartan kilts and fuzzy midriff knits in Empire Records to Cher and Dionne wearing their co-ord plaid blazers and skirts, American preppy has a sugariness that we don't see in our European counterparts.

Back in old Blighty, preppy takes on a melting pot of vibes. You can, quite rightly, go straight to Sloane Ranger ideals, but there is a collision in the culture that makes our North/South divide bind. This harps back to the aesthetic that Coco Chanel clung onto while in the Highlands. It's clothing for the countryside. In modern-day Britain, it's best viewed via the lens of a festival. Think muddy fields, unpredictable weather and clobber that has to look chic but be bloody practical. It's Alexa Chung, from Glastonbury to T in the Park. Beige and khaki waxed jackets and welly boots paired with the hint of a sharp collar under a funky knit. Chung is my quintessential British preppy muse.

With all this waterproofing, it should be no surprise for you to discover that waxed raincoats started life in Scotland. Charles Macintosh (not to be confused with his fellow Glaswegian namesake – the world-renowned architect with a slightly different spelling) made the Mac out of rubberised fabric. They first went on sale in 1824. Charles patented the idea after Scottish surgeon James Syme conducted a chemical experiment leading him to discover a valuable substance could be obtainable from coal tar, which has the property of dissolving India rubber and could be used for waterproofing silk and other textile fabrics. The Macintosh headquarters are still in Cumbernauld to this day. Synonymous with Humphrey Bogart, it's hard not to think of him standing in a trilby, dressed in a Mac, when conjuring thoughts of the overcoats. Thank God it rains so much in Scotland, without it we could have missed out on one of the world's most iconic coats.

Then of course there's Barbour, founded in 1894 by John Barbour, who was born and bred in Galloway in the Scottish Borders. His impact on chic cultural dressing lives on thanks to his daughter-in-law Dame Margaret Barbour and granddaughter Helen. Both women are responsible for taking this brand from the backs of fishermen to the spines of Sloane Rangers. Initially designed for seamen, river workers, motorcyclists and Royal Navy submariners, it is now a fashion staple that has graced the likes of James Bond, Steve McQueen, and the Royal family. It doesn't get more preppy than that, my friends.

The Welly Boot* Song

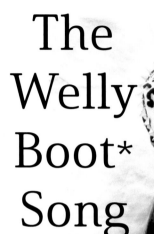

'If it wasnae fir yir wellies
where wid you be?
you'd be in some Halston
or even Mulberry
cause you wid have a dose
o the fashion
fab-U-lous
if it wissne fir yer feet in yer wellies!
Wellies they are wonderful
wellies they are swell
they keep out the watter
and they keep in the smell.
When you're sittin in a room
you can always tell when some
Buggar swaps their stiletto's fir their
wellies'

Sung to the tune of Sir Billy Connolly's
'The Welly Boot Song', originally written
by George McEwan.
*but make it fashion!

GOTHIC

ADJECTIVE

1. *a style of architecture that originated in France in the middle of the 12th century and spread throughout western Europe during the middle of the 16th century. typified by the use of pointed arches, ribbed vaults, flying buttresses and stained glass.*

NOUN

1. *the arts and crafts of the Gothic period.*

2. *the language of the Goths, Germanic in origin, now exctinct.*

3. *a piece of media in the gothic style.*

4. *black-letter typography or caligraphy with no serifs or hairlines.*

In Fashion

Gothic fashion is shown through dark, mysterious, antiquated and co-ordinating features. It is proudly worn in the Goth subculture.

Typical gothic fashion includes dyed black hair, dark 'bitten' lips and noir clothing in lace and velvets.

Styles are often borrowed from punk, Victorian and Elizabethan trends.

Not to be confused with heavy metal fashion or emo trends. There's a deeper connection to literature with this movement.

Skin tight inky fabric snuggly wound round the torso. The restrictive elegance of the garment so alluring to my childlike gaze.

Captivating my imagination was Anjelica Houston embodying Morticia Addams. As I ran around town in the '90s I presumed everyone must have been to the pictures to watch *The Addams Family* rather than understanding a movement rooted in my homeland. Union Street was choc-a-block with mystical macabre creatures queuing outside the Cathouse. Circling around the columns of GOMA the goths would gather like a conspiracy of ravens. In the five days allocated

to Scottish summer when the sun would scorch the street these souls would look so out of place, but for the other 360 days of the year our weather fed into their style aesthetic like they were all in gloomy cahoots. When I moved to Edinburgh as a teenager I discovered the haar. An eerie mist that rolls in off the Forth at the docks in Leith leaving its mark across all corners of the city. When it happens, you are instantly transported to the Edinburgh of Arthur Conan Doyle and Robert Louis Stevenson. You feel compelled to cloak yourself in gothic chic to lurk around the closes like the lassie in the Scottish Widows advert.

It's easy to see the impact the city had on our cultural forefathers spawning *Sherlock Holmes* and *Dr Jekyll and Mr Hyde*.

However, there is one woman who trumps all this, the matriarch of the gothic movement and the mother of modern horror: Ms Mary Shelley.

I came across this connection as a very green fresher, confused by a themed bar nestled in the heart of the Old Town, sporting Frankenstein's name. As it served me cheap chips and even cheaper cocktails, the link between this ubiquitous character and our capital city seemed far-fetched. So, my curious mind set off down the rabbit hole of research, abandoning my studies in search of something more satisfying. What I discovered was a Celtic connection bonding Shelley to Scottish shores, much like JK Rowling writing *Harry Potter* between the Balmoral and the coffee shop two doors down from said bar.

Now, the origins of *Frankenstein* go back a little further than Shelley's feverish dream in Switzerland. At the age of 14, she was sent to live with the Baxter family on the outskirts of Dundee. In the 1831 introduction to a revised edition of *Frankenstein*, she speaks fondly of her days by the River Tay:

'It was beneath the trees of the grounds belonging to our house, or on the bleak sides of the woodless mountains near, that my true compositions, the airy

flights of my imagination, were born and fostered.'

Parts of *Frankenstein* are set in Fife, Edinburgh and Orkney. In a rundown hut on Orkney, most notably, Victor creates – and destroys – the Bride, fearing the hideous race of creatures Frankenstein's monster and the Bride would produce.

In Fiona Sampson's book, *In Search of Mary Shelley: The Girl Who Wrote Frankenstein*, she writes extensively about Mary's time in Scotland and how her husband, Percy Bysshe Shelley, would describe her wearing bold tartan dresses in London in a bid to stand out from the crowd.

For me Alexander McQueen exemplifies our link between fashion and literature in the Gothic movement like no other label. Lee McQueens love affair with Scotland was most visual in his controversial 1995 collection Highland Rape. The inspiration for the show was based around his perception of England's rape of Scotland. The dark gothic undertones look like he had Mary Shelley as his ghost writer. But I will forever think of Lee dressed in formal highland wear standing beside Sarah Jessica Parker both wrapped in McQueen plaid at the foot of the steps of the Met Gala in 2006. The haunting beauty of the tartan combined with black lace and taupe tulle was a masterclass in Gothic dressing. Long live McQueen.

MARY
Shelley

FRANKENSTEIN

'A human being in perfection ought
always to preserve a calm and peaceful
mind and never to allow passion or a
transitory desire to disturb his tranquility.
I do not think that the pursuit of
knowledge is an exception to this rule.
If the study to which you apply yourself
has a tendency to weaken your affections
and to destroy your taste for those simple
pleasures in which no alloy can possibly
mix, then that study is certainly unlawful,
that is to say, not befitting the human
mind. If this rule were always observed; if
no man allowed any pursuit whatsoever
to interfere with the tranquillity of his
domestic affections, Greece had not
been enslaved, Caesar would have
spared his country, America would have
been discovered more gradually, and
the empires of Mexico and Peru had not
been destroyed.'

NED

non-educated delinquent

NOUN Derogatory

Scottish

1. *a hooligan or petty criminal.*

2. *a stupid or aggressive person.*

Think Begbie in *Trainspotting* as the poster child.

The evolution of the ned is an interesting one and coincides with the hijacking of some of our most prestigious Scottish textiles. Pringle had made the diamond motif knit an icon, adorning Hollywood stars, from Grace Kelly to James Dean, who looked divine wearing one in *East of Eden*. Worn by the film elite and sports stars alike, the print took to the skids, becoming an emblem associated with terrace fighting and binge drinking. Begbie became the pinnacle of the movement when *Trainspotting* debuted in cinemas.

Burberry too had the same dilemma. Their instantly recognisable tan tartan is a derivative of the Thomson check. And since tartan can be replicated, reproduced, redesigned and repurposed by using the smallest of set changes, anyone is free to wear and create similar structures without infringement. So, when the sporting casuals of the 1980s and 1990s adopted a Burberry-looking print as their own, we saw the withdrawal of the check with which Burberry became synonymous. It has taken several decades for the pattern to come back into circulation, proving one thing: fashion is always about timing.

ROYALTY

NOUN

1. *people of royal blood or status*

2. *a member of a royal family.*

3. *the most successful, famous or highly regarded members of a particular group.*

There are a handful of women in history who have the ability to change the fortunes of the British textiles industry simply by being themselves.

Naomi Campbell is one. I hereby declare my allegiance to her as my fashion Queen. I also propose she be elected Chief of Clan Campbell. Sorry, Torquhil Campbell – I know there have been clan fights started over less! For the past four decades, fixated eyes have followed her every footstep as she devoutly showcased the best our nation has to offer. A better global ambassador, I couldn't conjure. Any piece seen on our couture queen can sell out in moments.

As I began thinking about the themes of this book – punk to preppy, gothic to grunge, romance to royalty – it struck me that Naomi has been at the helm of each of these modern day fashion movements. Campbell has been the conductor of the cloth produced by my nation her whole career.

Those iconic blown-out-checks and enlarged houndstooths by her papa Azzedine Alaia, to the delightfully playful plaid tartan patchwork skirt suits of Gianni Versace, Campbell could nail all of theses trends in any given season.

From Burberry to Balmain, she has the ability to unite the crown the way Bonnie Prince Charlie never could. The young pretender too had powerful backers from

Paris to Rome in King Louis xv and Pope Clement xiii. You've got to love a little serendipitous synergy as heads in Paris (Alaia and Lagerfeld) and Rome (Versace, Gucci and Miu Miu) anointed her their queen, like those generations before did with our young Stuart.

In my mind's-eye she is forever draped in tartan finery from Vivienne Westwood.

The pair are a match made in heaven. The epitome of fashion royalty. It warms my cockles, as Dame Westwood has woven with us at DC Dalgliesh. She also uses another one of our great mills: Lochcarron of Scotland, who weave just down the road from us in Selkirk.

What is so interesting about Westwood and Campbell is their ability to blend punk and royalty so effortlessly throughout their careers. If I were to describe Westwood in fabric form, she would be tartan. A myriad of inter-weaving parallel lines that make up countless different patterns, using a kaleidoscope of colours while straddling two movements that should be at complete loggerheads with each other. One symbolising elitism and tradition; the other emblematic of disruption and anarchy. Vivienne deserves a book all to herself, and indeed Alexander Fury's in-depth tome on Britain's fashion matriarch is not to be missed for that very reason. She has done

what no other designer has managed to do, living in both movements at once. Her love of Scotland is something she is very vocal about and at times has landed her in hot water.

While picking up her 2014 Scottish Fashion Award, she threw her weight behind Scottish independence during her acceptance speech, which sent tongues wagging north and south of the border. It sparked fierce criticism from both camps. But let's be honest, it was a pretty punk thing to do. She also had a long-standing dispute with Harris Tweed over the use of the orb that both parties use as their logo. In highlighting Westwood, I want to explore the overlapping of two of the biggest trends we see on catwalks: punk and royalty.

Then there are our real royals. Princess Diana did what no other member of the palace had done before her, elevating designers onto a global stage and making them household names. Now, the Duchess of Cambridge comfortably bears that sartorial crown.

During the Queen's Diamond Jubilee procession, Kate took a leaf out of Her Majesty's style book and opted for a block colour. The Duchess looked radiant in head-to-toe red. However, there was a splash of tartan spiralled around her neck, breaking up the sea of crimson while sailing down the Thames. The scarf was woven in the Strathearn tartan: red, yellow and green

combined into a tight symmetrical set. The excitement back at the mill was palpable when the hand-knotting wafted elegantly around in the wind.

You see, that hand-knotting is the artisan jewel in our crown. Our calling card, if you like. She has worn it several times over the last decade in a nod to her Countess of Strathearn title, with each outing reverberating a positive ripple back to Selkirk. My personal favourite saw her style out the scarf while wearing head-to-toe camel. The Duchess broke up the colour block with a flash of tartan as she attended the opening of Balfour Hospital in Orkney.

I discussed the so-called 'Kate Effect' with Bethan Holt on an episode of my podcast *A Guide to Luxury*. For the last ten years, Bethan has reported on the Duchess' calendar for *The Telegraph*. In 2021 she released a book called *The Duchess of Cambridge: A Decade of Modern Royal Style*. I was astounded, but not surprised, to hear Bethan say the Duchess has boosted the British fashion industry by up to £1 billion in a single year.

From the hands of the artisans to the *décolletage* of our future Queen, the economy of fabric feeds families across our nation. I'm thrilled to have such an incredible female ambassador in the Duchess – and I'm even more inspired by the thoughtful outfit choices that always showcase the best of British.

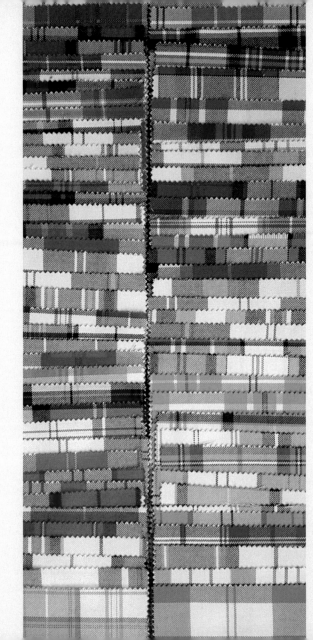

However, this union between royalty and my nation's national dress hasn't always been so harmonious. And the origins of this trend are rooted in a conflict that dates back centuries – the Jacobite uprising of 1745, which led to the banning of tartan being worn. But the cultural, economic and political movings of the Crown before this date are the seeds sown for such a revolution. James VI and I – Mary, Queen of Scots' son – ascended the throne after the death of the woman who had his own mother executed when he was an infant, Queen Elizabeth I. To be fair, her chances of normality were never really achievable since her father, Henry VIII had her own mother beheaded when she was a child. Anyway, I think we are all familiar with this famous family's misdemeanours, so I shall not digress. With all this crown-hopping and head-lopping, sections of the country were splintered off. Ultimately, sectarianism was at the root of all the infighting. Sadly, we are still blighted by this today, centuries on. It's the plaid that wraps itself around each warring party now, as it did then.

Less than a hundred years later, the Rising and its aftermath became fertile ground for writers romanticising war stories. It's where we find a social-climbing Sir Walter Scott at his most aggressive, wooing the Crown to project a new Scotland to show the world – an image that has been lapped up, even to this day. And it's the birth of what I like to dub 'modern tartan'.

King George IV came to visit Edinburgh in 1822. Bridges were erected, dinners were had and the New Town was built. Despite Sir Walter's downright racist views on King George's mother, the pair forged a relationship that would set royalty's tartan tone for the next two centuries. Suddenly, tartan was back with a bang and on the backs of royals, less than a century after being banned.

Fifteen years later, Queen Victoria would up the tartan ante when she inherited the throne. At the tender age of 18, her father's three elder brothers died without leaving legitimate offspring. However, William IV was survived by eight of the ten illegitimate children he'd sired. Now how's that for juicy family gossip?

Sweeping away the decadence of regency splendour, Victoria wanted her reign to adopt a more prudent approach. But there was one thing that would remain, and that was the romancing of Alba. Balmoral became the beloved home for Victoria and Albert and they set about plaiding anything that could be pinned down. Albert went on to design the official Balmoral tartan – a rather dreary grey offering with a lightning bolt of red through it to break up the monotony. It was said to represent the shimmery grey stone of the Granite City, as Balmoral falls inside Aberdeenshire. However, it failed to capture the sparkle of the stone, instead harnessing the harshness of the Victorian era.

The royals still use the tartan today, and they are very protective over who can wear it and how it is reproduced. It is only authorised to be worn by the royal household.

And although Victoria and Albert gave good plaid, there's another design king and queen of Scotland who thoroughly deserve their crowns. They are Christopher Kane and Hayley Scanlan. They define what it means to be Scottish, but have international hitting-power without a hint of chintz in sight.

As I wrap up on royalty there is one final thought I want to share about the Balmoral tartan. That is, despite the royal household's chokehold on Prince Albert's designs, tartan has a way of smashing establishment rules. As I have said before, tartan can be woven in any shade, set and size. Slight tweaks to any design mean a new tartan can be born. There are a myriad of similar tartans in slate grey, red and black. You can even go ahead and design your own variation. Tartan can't be tamed; it can be woven any which way you want. Proving it's the most punk material on the planet.

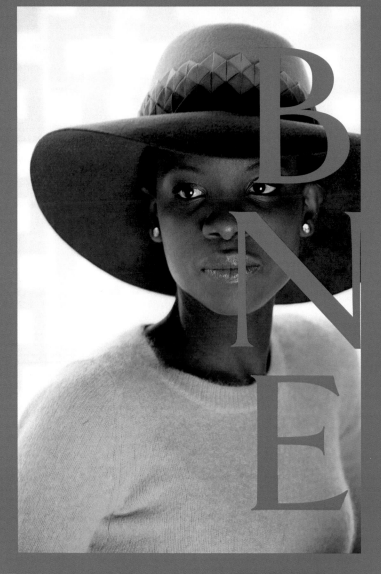

BUNNET

Pronounced like punnet.

Scottish

1. *a head covering, can be a hat or a cap.*

WORD ORIGIN

Old French, *'chapel de bonet'*

A word that dates back several centuries, a bunnet is most commonly known as a flat, brimless hat for men (although it did, at one time, refer to a woman's hat as well, as Robert Burns' 'To a Louse' attests). My grandfather never left the house without his. Come hail, rain or shine that weathered tweed cap resided firmly on his beautiful baldy napper.

The bunnet has survived and thrived in Scottish culture since the 14th century, where its first usage was found and recorded.

Much more than a piece of headgear, the bunnet was, for a long time, a signifier of social status. It has also been an integral part of the Scottish infantry uniform. Its wide application in Scottish civil and military society has prolonged its presence atop the heads of working men, armed forces personnel and fashionistas alike.

My bunnet of choice is cashmere, of course.

Ye ugly, creepin, blastit wonner,
Detested, shunn'd by saunt an' sinner,
How daur ye set your fit upon her –
Sae fine a lady?
Gae somewhere else and seek your dinner
On some poor body.

Swith! in some beggar's haffet squattle;
There ye may creep, and sprawl, and sprattle,
Wi' ither kindred, jumping cattle,
In shoals and nations;
Whaur horn nor bane ne'er daur unsettle
Your thick plantations.

Now haud you there, ye're out o' sight,
Below the fatt'rels, snug and tight;
Na, faith ye yet! ye'll no be right,
Till ye've got on it –
The verra tapmost, tow'rin height
O' Miss' bonnet.

Robert Burns

PUNK

NOUN

1. *a loud, and aggressive form of popular music, set to a fast tempo, popular in the late 1970s.*

2. *a worthless person, used as an abusive word in North America*

3. *a criminal or troublemaker.*

Punk is the most peacock of our trends. It takes a lot of effort to conform to this crusade. Its core is about ideology, the concept of personal freedom and anti-establishment. This is about research, questioning the status quo and a belief that you can change things you are unhappy with by not conforming – creating a way of life for yourself.

Here in the UK, Vivienne Westwood and the Sex Pistols are synonymous with the movement. Over time they became the figureheads that history hangs its hat on. This statement alone is tinged with controversy as this subculture isn't searching for a leader.

And although the backdrop of economic struggles and a generation suffering with the post-war slump was a breeding ground for punk, this isn't where it all began.

I have touched upon the rebellion of 1745 throughout this book, as its significance is tangled up in more than dreams of a liberated Scotland. But no story begins with a fight. There is always a build-up, and Scotland has that in abundance.

For a greater understanding, we have to dig a little deeper. So, I'll skip the needle back on this record another 200 years to tell you the trilogy of the Jameses. The house of Stewart is by far our most successful Scottish monarchy period. James IV, perceived to be the most successful Stewart, inadvertently killed his father after becoming the figurehead of a second rebellion that resulted in the Battle of Sauchieburn, where his father fell. He wore the guilt around his waist each Lent, wrapping a heavy iron chain cilice next to his skin. Annually, he would add an extra ounce of weight to numb the mental pain. He would suffer the same fate as his father at the Battle of Flodden, becoming the last British monarch to be killed in battle. His one-year-old son would become King, only avenging Henry VIII via his grandson.

James I and VI would ascend the throne after Queen Elizabeth died childless, ending the Tudors' run, meaning the Scottish and English crowns were finally unified. I'll clarify any confusion: James VI was the great grandson of King Henry VII. And of course, as I mentioned before, Queen Elizabeth killed James' mother, Mary, Queen of Scots, who was her cousin. Now, how's that for family in-fighting?

This is where religion, politics and power collide. As the Reformation ripped through Europe, the kings and queens in each part of the realm were losing their heads – literally. Now, your Jacobean knowledge may be a little sketchy, but I'm betting you will definitely know about Bonfire Night on the 5th of November. Well, James I and VI was the king that the anti-establishment wanted to blow up. Guy Fawkes was an Englishman of Catholic faith who wanted to bring down the Protestant monarch. This was despite James I being a Protestant whose mother was Catholic (Mary, Queen of Scots) and his hopes had been not only to unify the Scottish and English Crowns, but also to heal the rift between Catholics and Protestants living across the country.

It still makes me feel a little squeamish that we burn effigies of Guy every year and celebrate his murder with a giant fireworks display. I much prefer my million pounds-worth of gunpowder going off on Hogmanay or at the end of the Edinburgh Festival.

Now, I have told you how plaid has played its role in all of this. The rebels of 1745 wore tartan into battle to fight the establishment. It was then banned from being worn before it was reinstated by George IV. But it is this nod to anti-establishment that the punk movement from the 1970s understood well and why it adopted tartan into its uniform.

That's how deliberate-looking punk is. Out of every trend we see, each genre gives a snapshot into the individual's innermost thoughts. They are displayed on the body like a textile tableau. Punk is the epitome of this.

THEY ARE
EACH OTHER'S
YIN AND YANG.

THE

GOONIE

pronounced goo-knee

1. *a dressing gown or housecoat.*

Not to be confused with the cult classic kids movie from the 1980s

Hands down my favourite item of clothing. They come in many forms, shapes, patterns and sizes but the one overriding rule is it must be COMFORTABLE.

This word is best used nestled in beside other Scottish words:

'Come coorie in and get cozy in your goonie.'

This means cuddle up and get comfortable wrapped in your nightgown.

My kids curl up in mine and I steal my husband's. It's a universal robe that just feels like a fabric hug. When I had my cashmere business, the wrap became the best-selling item out of the six capsule jumpers I'd put together. It wasn't lost on me, I had researched enough to know that I wanted a garment you could wear outside and in bed. There is nothing more luxurious than getting covered up in a giant cashmere wrap. I wear mine to the beach when it's chilly and dress up my fancy one for nights out, but ultimately my favourite way to wear it is in bed.

IT'S TIME TO SLEEP
ALL THE WAY
THROUGH THE NIGHT
UNTIL THE SUN
COMES UP
IN YOUR BIG BOY BED
WITH NO MORE
BOOBIES
UNTIL TOMORROW
MORNING

A bedtime tale given to each of my sons as babies – Lynne Coleman.

GOOD NIGHT

OIDHCHE MHATH

PICTURE CREDITS

Every image and illustration in this book is work that I created or commissioned on different projects with creative teams over the past decade.

page 6: Josh Kilimanjaro is photographed for The Shepherd's Plaid Project by Lynne Coleman for DC Dalgliesh.

page 11: Lynne Coleman photograph by Jane Barlow.

page 12-21: all images are copyright of Isolated Heroes.

page 24: illustration by Katie Braid.

page 24: all images by Lynne Coleman.

page 27: Claire & Adam wrapped in Shepherds Plaids photography by Lynne Coleman.

pages 29, 30 & 36: image by Lynne Coleman.

pages 32, 35 and 37: Lynne wears vintage wedding gown image by Aleksandra Modrzejewska.

pages 38, 40, 42, 43: Rachel photographed by Nuala Swan for Crave. Make-up by Molly Jane Sheridan.

page 44: illustration by Katie Braid.

pages 46, 56 & 57: Jude styled by Alexandra Fiddes, photography by Igor Termenón for Crave.

pages 48 & 51: Robyn, Georgia & Lili styled by Katie Connelly, photography by Brian Sweeney, make up by Molly Jane Sheridan for CrossCashmere.

page 52: love illustration by Lynne Coleman.

page 55: Lili styled by Katie Connelly, photography by Brian Sweeney, make up by Molly Jane Sheridan for CrossCashmere.

page 58: Lynne Coleman, photography courtesy of Pringle of Scotland.

page 60: Tom for ROX magazine, image courtesy of ROX photography by Brian Sweeney.

page 62: illustration by Katie Braid.

pages 64: Robyn, Lili, Georgia & Josh for CrossCashmere photography by Brian Sweeney. Make-up by Molly Jane Sheridan. Styled by Katie Connelly.

page 66: illustration by Katie Braid.

page 68: Grace Kelly wearing Pringle of Scotland illustrated by Lynne Coleman.

page 70: illustration by Katie Braid.

page 72: Coco Chanel illustrated by Lynne Coleman.

pages 76-78: Sophie wears Pringle of Scotland with Obscure Couture for Scotland Re:Designed, photography by Brian Sweeney. Make-up Alexis Miller.

pages 81: Lynne Coleman photography by Aleksandra Modrzejewska.

pages 82 & 83: Lynne Coleman wearing Mulberry for Crave, photography by Stew Bryden, make-up by Molly Jane Sheridan.

page 84: Alexander McQueen Spring 2011 illustrated by Katie Braid.

page 86: Lynne Coleman wearing Max Mara for Crave, photography by Stew Bryden, make-up by Molly Jane Sheridan.

pages 88 & 90: images for *The Fashion Annual*, photography by Christina Kernohan, model Katie Connelly. Make-up by Molly Jane Sheridan. With thanks to Glasgow University for the venue.

page 92: Lynne Coleman self portrait.

page 94: Lynne Coleman wearing Max Mara for Crave, photography by Stew Bryden, make-up by Molly Jane Sheridan.

page 96-97: photograph by Lynne Coleman.

page 98: Begby on oil and watercolour illustrated by Lynne Coleman.

page 100: Robyn, Charles, Lili, Georgia & Josh for CrossCashmere photography by Brian Sweeney. Make-up by Molly Jane Sheridan. Styled by Katie Connelly.

page 102: illustration of The Duchess of Cambridge by Katie Braid.

page 104: illustration of Naomi Campbell by Lynne Coleman.

page 106: images by Lynne Coleman.

page 108 Lynne Colman photography by Aleksandra Modrzejewska.

page 110: image courtesy of ROX photography by Brian Sweeney.

page 112: image by Katie Braid for DC Dalgliesh.

page 114-115: tartan samples images by Lynne Coleman for DC Dalgliesh.

page 116: Numba wearing Sally Ann Provan hat, image courtesy of Sally Ann Provan, Photography Alistair Clark.

page 117: Lynne Coleman photography by Jane Barlow.

page 118: Simone wears CrossCashmere, photography by Lynne Coleman.

page 119: model wears Obscure Couture for Crave, photography by Martin Barker. Headpiece by Molly Jane Sheridan.

page 122: Katy at Superior Model Management for Crave, photography Stewart Bryden, make-up Molly Jane Sheridan, hair Anna Wade.

page 123: Natasha for ROX Magazine, image courtesy of ROX. Photography by Bethany Grace. Make-up by Molly Jane Sheridan.

page 124: Stephen wears cashmere beanie, photography by Lynne Coleman.

page 126: punk illustration by Katie Braid.

page 128: photography by Brian Sweeney, styled by Lynne Coleman, make-up Alexis Miller.

pages 130, 131, 132 & 139: Lyndsey & Jenn founders of Obscure Couture, photography by Brian Sweeney, styled by Lynne Coleman, make-up by Alexis Miller for Scotland Re:Designed.

pages 134 & 136: Georgia for Crave, photography by Christina Kernohan.

page 140: illustration by Lynne Coleman.

pages 142 & 143: photography by Brian Sweeney, styled by Lynne Coleman, make-up Alexis Miller for Scotland Re:Designed.

page 144: image by Lynne Coleman.

page 145: Lynne Colman photography by Aleksandra Modrzejewska.

pages 146 & 147: Robyn, Charles, Lili, Georgia & Josh for CrossCashmere photography by Brian Sweeney. Make-up by Molly Jane Sheridan.

page 148: image by Lynne Coleman.

page 150: Josh Kilimanjaro is photographed for The Shepherd's Plaid Project by Lynne Coleman for DC Dalgliesh.

ACKNOWLEDGEMENTS

With thanks to the incredible team at Luath. Bravo Eilidh for whipping this book into shape. To Morv for working your word magic, I rely on you for much more than spelling. Here's to the next 20 years!

Thank you to all the creatives I've collaborated with over the years.

Kim & Eve you are wonder women. Thank you for being the consummate professionals you are and looking devastating while you do so.

Katie, these beautiful illustrations are only a snippet of your unbelievable talent. Thank you for painting them & allowing them to be in the book. I thank the heavens daily that I have you in my world.

Gilly, what a year we've had. Thank you for your unwavering support. Here's to being each other's biggest cheerleader.

Big Guy, three kids and three books in, thank you for being the facilitator of dreams in all aspects of life. I love you.

And finally...

Gabriel, Rafe & Ruben this is what I was doing in-between our summer of bay hopping, sea swimming and island exploring. My babies, may your lives always be about beaches and boats.

Luath Press Limited

committed to publishing well written books worth reading

LUATH PRESS takes its name from Robert Burns, whose little collie Luath (*Gael.*, swift or nimble) tripped up Jean Armour at a wedding and gave him the chance to speak to the woman who was to be his wife and the abiding love of his life. Burns called one of the 'Twa Dogs' Luath after Cuchullin's hunting dog in Ossian's *Fingal*. Luath Press was established in 1981 in the heart of Burns country, and is now based a few steps up the road from Burns' first lodgings on Edinburgh's Royal Mile. Luath offers you distinctive writing with a hint of unexpected pleasures.

Most bookshops in the UK, the US, Canada, Australia, New Zealand and parts of Europe, either carry our books in stock or can order them for you. To order direct from us, please send a £sterling cheque, postal order, international money order or your credit card details (number, address of cardholder and expiry date) to us at the address below. Please add post and packing as follows: UK – £1.00 per delivery address; overseas surface mail – £2.50 per delivery address; overseas airmail – £3.50 for the first book to each delivery address, plus £1.00 for each additional book by airmail to the same address. If your order is a gift, we will happily enclose your card or message at no extra charge.

Luath Press Limited
543/2 Castlehill
The Royal Mile
Edinburgh EH1 2ND
Scotland
Telephone: +44 (0)131 225 4326 (24 hours)
email: sales@luath. co.uk
Website: www. luath.co.uk